QUOTES

OF

MICHAEL JACKSON

Inspirational & Motivational

Quotes

of

Michael Jackson

Quotations by Michael Jackson, American Musician,

Born August 29, 1958.

Michael Joseph Jackson was an American singer, songwriter, record producer, dancer, and actor.

Terms Of Use Agreement

Every effort had been made to fulfill requirements with regard to reproducing copyrighted material. The author and the publisher will be glad to certify any omissions at the earliest opportunity.

Disclaimer

Quotes of the King of Pop

Let us dream of tomorrow where we can truly love from the soul, and know love as the ultimate truth at the heart of all creation.
— Michael Jackson

My mother's wonderful. To me she's perfection.
— Michael Jackson

I don't understand why the press is so interested in speculating about my appearance, anyway. What does my face have to do with my music or my dancing?
— Michael Jackson

But I will never stop helping and loving people the way Jesus said to.
— Michael Jackson

Children show me in their playful smiles the divine in everyone. This simple goodness shines straight from their hearts and only asks to be loved.
— Michael Jackson

Well, you don't get to do things that other children get to do, having friends and slumber parties and buddies. There were none of that for me. I didn't have friends when I was little. My brothers were my friends.
— Michael Jackson

They did it to try and belittle me, to try and to take away my pride. But I went through the whole system with them. And at the end, I - I wanted the public to know that I was okay, even though I was hurting.
— Michael Jackson

You know, let's put it this way, if all the people in Hollywood who have had plastic surgery, if they went on vacation, there wouldn't be a person left in town.
— Michael Jackson

I'm a black American, I am proud of my race. I am proud of who I am. I have a lot of pride and dignity.
— Michael Jackson

The greatest education in the world is watching the masters at work.
— Michael Jackson

Because I think every child star suffers through this period because you're not the cute and charming child that you were. You start to grow, and they want to keep you little forever.
— Michael Jackson

Just because it's in print doesn't mean it's the gospel.
— Michael Jackson

I'm happy to be alive, I'm happy to be who I am.
— Michael Jackson

Elizabeth Taylor is gorgeous, beautiful, and she still is today, I'm crazy about her.
— Michael Jackson

I just wish I could understand my father.
— Michael Jackson

Because I wanted to have a place that I could create everything that I that I never had as a child. So, you see rides. You see animals. There's a movie theater.
— Michael Jackson

It's a complete lie, why do people buy these papers? It's not the truth I'm here to say. You know, don't judge a person, do not pass judgement, unless you have talked to them one on one. I don't care what the story is, do not judge them because it is a lie.

— Michael Jackson

I'm just like anyone. I cut and I bleed. And I embarass easily.

— Michael Jackson

If you enter this world knowing you are loved and you leave this world knowing the same, then everything that happens in between can be dealt with.

— Michael Jackson

The meaning of life is contained in every single expression of life. It is present in the infinity of forms and phenomena that exist in all of creation.

— Michael Jackson

When I see children, I see the face of God. That's why I love them so much. That's what I see.
— Michael Jackson

People write negatives things, cause they feel that's what sells. Good news to them, doesn't sell.
— Michael Jackson

I'm never pleased with anything, I'm a perfectionist, it's part of who I am.
— Michael Jackson

Yes, and I had pimples so badly it used to make me so shy. I used not to look at myself. I'd hide my face in the dark, I wouldn't want to look in the mirror and my father teased me and I just hated it and I cried everyday.
— Michael Jackson

Everything that I love is behind those gates. We have elephants, and giraffes, and crocodiles, and every kind of tigers and lions. And - and we have bus loads of kids,

who don't get to see those things. They come up sick children, and enjoy it.
— Michael Jackson

Why can't you share your bed? The most loving thing to do is to share your bed with someone. It's very charming. It's very sweet. It's what the whole world should do.
— Michael Jackson

Well, especially now I come to realize - and then - I would do my schooling which was three hours with a tutor and right after that I would go to the recording studio and record, and I'd record for hours and hours until it's time to go to sleep.
— Michael Jackson

Before I would hurt a child, I would slit my wrists.
— Michael Jackson

Me and Janet really are two different people.
— Michael Jackson

And I remember going to the record studio and there was a park across the street and I'd see all the children playing and I would cry because it would make me sad that I would have to work instead.

— Michael Jackson

I will say again that I have never, and would never, harm a child. It sickens me that people have written untrue things about me.

— Michael Jackson

Everyone who knows me will know the truth, which is that my children come first in my life and that I would never harm any child.

— Michael Jackson

I love my family very much. I wish I could see them a little more often than I do. But we understand because we're a show business family and we all work.

— Michael Jackson

Because parents have power over children. They feel they have to do what their parents say. But the love of money is the root of all evil. And this is a sweet child.

And to see him turn like this, this isn't him. This is not him.
— Michael Jackson

I was a veteran, before I was a teenager.
— Michael Jackson

There were times when I had great times with my brothers, pillow fights and things, but I was, used to always cry from loneliness.
— Michael Jackson

The Bee Gees who are brilliant, I just love great music.
— Michael Jackson

Please keep an open mind and let me have my day in court.
— Michael Jackson

I remember one time we were getting ready to go to South America and everything was packed up and in the car ready to go and I hid and I was crying because I

really did not want to go, I wanted to play. I did not want to go.
— Michael Jackson

Well Brooke, I've always liked her, and when I was little I used to stay with Diana Ross, me and my brothers stayed with her for years and I never said, but I always had a crush on her.
— Michael Jackson

I have a skin disorder that destroys the pigmentation of my skin, it's something that I cannot help, OK?
— Michael Jackson

Yeah, Wacko Jacko, where did that come from? Some English tabloid. I have a heart and I have feelings. I feel that when you do that to me. It's not nice.
— Michael Jackson

I've helped many, many, many children, thousands of children, cancer kids, leukemia kids.
— Michael Jackson

In a world filled with hate, we must still dare to hope. In a world filled with anger, we must still dare to comfort. In a world filled with despair, we must still dare to dream. And in a world filled with distrust, we must still dare to believe.
— Michael Jackson

If you enter this world knowing you are loved and you leave this world knowing the same, then everything that happens in between can be dealt with.
— Michael Jackson

Lies run sprints, but the truth runs marathons.
— Michael Jackson

When they say the sky's the limit to me that's really true
— Michael Jackson

We have to heal our wounded world. The chaos, despair, and senseless destruction we see today are a result of the alienation that people feel from each other and their environment.
— Michael Jackson

To live is to be musical, starting with the blood dancing in your veins. Everything living has a rhythm. Do you feel your music?

— Michael Jackson

People ask me how I make music. I tell them I just step into it. It's like stepping into a river and joining the flow. Every moment in the river has its song.

— Michael Jackson

Hope is such a beautiful word, but it often seems very fragile. Life is still being needlessly hurt and destroyed.

— Michael Jackson

All of us are products of our childhood.

— Michael Jackson

In their innocence, very young children know themselves to be light and love. If we will allow them, they can teach us to see ourselves the same way.

— Michael Jackson

When children listen to music, they don't just listen. They melt into the melody and flow with the rhythm. Something inside starts to unfold its wings - soon the child and the music are one.
— Michael Jackson

To give someone a piece of your heart, is worth more than all the wealth in the world.
— Michael Jackson

Sometimes the heart is so heavy that we turn away from it and forget that its throbbing is the wisest message of life, a wordless message that says, Live, be, move, rejoice -- you are alive! Without the heart's wise rhythm, we could not exist.
— Michael Jackson

When I step out on stage in front of thousands of people, I don't feel that I'm being brave. It can take much more courage to express true feelings to one person. [...] In spite of the risks, the courage to be honest and intimate opens the way to self-discovery. It offers what we all want, the promise of love.
— Michael Jackson

A star can never die. It just turns into a smile and melts back into the cosmic music, the dance of life.
— Michael Jackson

I love to read. I wish I could advise more people to read. There's a whole new world in books. If you can't afford to travel, you travel mentally through reading. You can see anything and go any place you want to in reading.
— Michael Jackson

Children show me in their playful smiles the divine in everyone.
— Michael Jackson

But for me the sweetest contact with God has no form. I close my eyes, look within, and enter a deep soft silence. The infinity of God's creation embraces me.
— Michael Jackson

And that's what innocence is. It's simple and trusting like a child, not judgmental and committed to one narrow point of view. If you are locked into a pattern of

thinking and responding, your creativity gets blocked. You miss the freshness and magic of the moment. Learn to be innocent again, and that freshness never fades.
— Michael Jackson

I'm just like anyone. I cut and I bleed and I embarrass easily.
— Michael Jackson

I'm going to search for my star until I find it. It's hidden in the drawer of innocence, wrapped in a scarf of wonder.
— Michael Jackson

They say that parenting is like dancing. You take one step, your child takes another.
— Michael Jackson

Look beyond yourself..
— Michael Jackson

Before you judge me , try hard to love me , look within your heart. Then ask , - have you seen my childhood ?
— Michael Jackson

But I will never stop helping and loving people the way Jesus said to.
— Michael Jackson

You're a vegetable!
— Michael Jackson

When all life is seen as divine, everyone grows wings.
— Michael Jackson

Each song is a child I nourish and give my love to. But even if you have never written a song, your life is a song. How can it not be?
— Michael Jackson

Please go for your dreams. Whatever your ideals, you can become whatever you want to become.
— Michael Jackson

Human knowledge consists not only of libraries of parchment and ink - it is also comprised of the volumes of knowledge that are written on the human heart,

chiselled on the human soul, and engraved on the human psyche.
— Michael Jackson

I'm really very self-confident when it comes to my work. When I take on a project, I believe in it 100%. I really put my soul into it. I'd die for it. That's how I am.
— Michael Jackson

You can't hurt me, I found peace within myself.
— Michael Jackson

I believe I'm one of the loneliest people in the world.
— Michael Jackson

Before you Judge me, Try hard to Love me
— Michael Jackson

I trembled to think of a world without stars. No guide for the sailor to trust at see, no jewels to dazzle our sense of beauty [...] But all around the globe, the air is so dirty and the lights from the cities are so bright that for some people few stars can be seen anymore. A

generation of children may grow up seeing a blank sky and asking, Did there used to be stars there?
— Michael Jackson

If you want to make the world a better place, take a look at yourself, and make a change.
— Michael Jackson

But they told me a man should be faithful, and walk when not able, and fight till the end but I'm only Human.
— Michael Jackson

The Wizard Of Oz has secrets that are just too much. Or Peter Pan – the whole 'lost boys' thing is just incredible. They're not childlike at all, they're really, really deep; you can rule your life by them. Or say 'child-like', because children are the most brilliant people of all, that's why they relate to those stories so well. Fairy-tales are wonderful.
— Michael Jackson

You are not alone.
— Michael Jackson

Lies run sprints, but the truth runs marathons. The truth will win this marathon in court.
— Michael Jackson

When you're strong and good, then you're Bad.
— Michael Jackson

The greatest education in the world is watching the masters at work
— Michael Jackson

Its all for love... L.O.V.E.
— Michael Jackson

All the things I've read in my school books about England and the Queen were okay, but my eyes are the greatest book in the world.
— Michael Jackson

In a world filled with hate, we must still dare to hope. In a world filled with anger, we must still dare to comfort. In a world filled with despair, we must still dare to

dream. And in a world filled with distrust, we must still dare to believe..
— Michael Jackson

Don't blame it on the sunshine. Don't blame it on the moonlight. Blame it on the boogie.
— Michael Jackson

I wrote a book called 'Dancing The Dream'. It was more autobiographical than Moonwalk, which I did with Mrs. Onassis. It wasn't full of gossip and scandal and all that trash that people write, so I don't think people paid much attention to it, but it came from my heart. It was essays, thoughts and things that I've thought about while on tour
— Michael Jackson

you give me fever from miles around
ill pick you up in my car and well paint the toown
— Michael Jackson

There's a whole psychological reason for those cartoons about good against evil. We have Superman and all those other hero people, so that we can go out into life

and try to be something. I've got most of Disney's animated movies on video-tapes, and when we watch them. Oh, I could just eat it, eat it. [...] Jimmy Cricket, Pinocchio, Mickey Mouse – these are world-known characters. Some of the greatest political figures have come to the United States to meet them.
— Michael Jackson

Often people just don't see what I see. They have too much doubt. You can't do your best when you're doubting yourself. If you don't believe in yourself, who will?
— Michael Jackson

In the field I'm in, there is a lot of that and it gets offered to me all the time. People even go as far as to just stick it in your pocket and walk off. Now, if it was a good thing, they wouldn't do that. I mean, would somebody drop something beautiful in my pocket and just walk off? But I don't want to have anything to do with any of that. I mean, as corny as it sounds, but this is how I really believe: Natural highs are the greatest highs in the world. Who wants to take something and just sit around for the rest of the day after you take it

(drugs), and don't know who you are, what you're doing, where you are? Take in something that's gonna inspire you to do greater things in the world.
— Michael Jackson

Everyone's Taking Control Of Me Seems That The World's Got A Role For Me I'm So Confused Will You Show To Me You'll Be There For Me And Care Enough To Bear Me
— Michael Jackson

I fast every Sunday. I don't eat anything. Just juices. [...] It flushes out the system, cleans out the colon. I think that's great. To really make it work, you have to do it properly. That's the sewer valve of the system. You have to keep that clean like you clean the outside of your body. All these impurities come out of your system because you're not clean inside. It comes out in pimples or disease or through big pores. Toxins trying to get out of your system. People should try to keep themselves clean.
— Michael Jackson

If all of the people in Hollywood had plastic surgery and went on vacation, there wouldn't be a person left in town.
— Michael Jackson

What happened to truth? Did it go out of style?
— Michael Jackson

In the end, the most important thing is to be true to yourself and those you love and work hard. I mean, work like there's no tomorrow. Train. Strive. I mean, really train and cultivate your talent to the highest degree. Be the best at what you do. Get to know more about your field than anybody alive. Use the tools of your trade, if it's books or a floor to dance on or a body of water to swim in. Whatever it is, it's yours.
— Michael Jackson

Once at a record store in San Francisco, over a thousand kids showed up. They pushed forward and broke a window. A big piece of glass fell on top of this girl. And the girl's throat was slit. She just got slit. And I remember there was blood everywhere. Oh God, so much blood. And she grabbed her throat and was

bleeding and everyone just ignored her. Why? Because I was there and they wanted to grab at me and get my autograph. I wonder whatever happened to that girl.
— Michael Jackson

I hate it. I hate taxidermy shops and all that crap.
— Michael Jackson

I'm really very self-confident when it comes to my work. When I take on a project, I believe in it 100%. I really put my soul into it. I'd die for it. That's how I am
— Michael Jackson

I'm a perfectionist; I'll work until I drop.
— Michael Jackson

My attitude is if fashion says it's forbidden, I'm going to do it.
— Michael Jackson

Just doing as well as you did last time is not good enough.
— Michael Jackson

I prefer just being with people I like. That's my way of celebrating.
— Michael Jackson

Stop this agony of wishing Play it out Don't think, don't hesitate Curving back within yourself Just create... Just create
— Michael Jackson

It always surprises me when people assume that something an artist has created is based on a true experience or reflects his or her own lifestyle. Often nothing could be farther from the truth. [...] An artist's imagination is his greatest tool. It can create a mood or feeling that people want to have, as well as transport you to a different place altogether.
— Michael Jackson

I'm starting with the man in the mirror
— Michael Jackson

In many ways an artist is his work. It's difficult to separate the two. I think I can be brutally objective about my work as I create it, and if something doesn't

work, I can feel it, but when I turn in a finished album — or song — you can be sure that I've given it every ounce of energy and God-given talent that I have.
— Michael Jackson

I remember going swimming as a child and making a wish before I jumped into the pool. [...] I'd stretch my arms out, as if I were sending my thoughts right into space. I'd make my wish, then I'd dive into the water. I'd say to myself, This is my dream. This is my wish, every time before I'd dive into the water.
— Michael Jackson

Whenever I saw a sunset, I would quietly make my secret wish right before the sun tucked under the western horizon and disappeared. It would seem as if the sun had taken my wish with it. I'd make it right before the last speck of light vanished.
— Michael Jackson

You can pray to the angels and they will listen, but the best way to call them, I am told, is to laugh. Angels respond to delight, because that is what they are made

of. In fact, when peoples minds are clouded by anger or hatred, no angel can reach them.
— Michael Jackson

It's easy to mistake being innocent for being simpleminded or naive. We all want to seem sophisticated; we all want to seem street-smart. To be innocent is to be out of it.
— Michael Jackson

Yet there is a deep truth in innocence. A baby looks in his mother's eyes, and all he sees is love. As innocence fades away, more complicated things take its place. We think we need to outwit others and scheme to get what we want. We begin to spend a lot of energy protecting ourselves. Then life turns into a struggle. People have no choice but to be street-smart. How else can they survive?
— Michael Jackson

When you get right down to it, survival means seeing things the way they really are and responding. It means being open. And that's what innocence is. It's simple and trusting like a child, not judgmental and committed to one narrow point of view. If you are locked into a pattern of thinking and responding, your creativity gets blocked. You miss the freshness and magic of the moment. Learn to be innocent again, and that freshness never fades.

— Michael Jackson

It 's strange that God doesn't mind expressing Himself/Herself in all the religions of the world, while people still cling to the notion that their way is the only right way. Whatever you try to say about God, someone will take offense, even if you say everyone's love of God is right for them. For me the form God takes is not the most important thing. What's most important is the essence. My songs and dances are outlines for Him to come in and fill. I hold out the form. She puts in the sweetness.

— Michael Jackson

What we need to learn from children isn't childish. Being with them connects us to the deep wisdom of life, which is ever present and only asks to be lived. Now, when the world is so confused and its problems so complicated, I feel we need our children more than

ever. Their natural wisdom points the way to solutions that lie, waiting to be recognized, within our own hearts.
— Michael Jackson

This world we live in is the dance of the creator. Dancers come and go in the twinkling of an eye, but the dance lives on.
— Michael Jackson

I can't think of a better way to spread the message of world peace than by working with the NFL and being part of Super Bowl XXVII.
— Michael Jackson

I don't like pop music.
— Michael Jackson

I'll always be Peter Pan in my heart.
— Michael Jackson

People think they know me, but they don't. Not really. Actually, I am one of the loneliest people on this earth. I

cry sometimes, because it hurts. It does. To be honest, I guess you could say that it hurts to be me.
— Michael Jackson

Just because you read it in a magazine or see it on a TV screen doesn't make it factual. To buy it is to feed it. - about tabloid magazines.
— Michael Jackson

I made a terrible mistake. I got caught up in the excitement of the moment. I would never intentionally endanger the lives of my children.
— Michael Jackson

You ain't seen nothing yet, and the best is yet to come. (1999)
— Michael Jackson

There is a lot of sadness in my past life. My father beat me. It was difficult to take being beaten and then going on stage. He was strict; very hard and stern.
— Michael Jackson

Elizabeth Taylor used to feed me, to hand-feed me, at times. Please, I don't want anybody to think I'm starving, I'm not. My health is perfect, actually.
— Michael Jackson

I just want to say to fans in every corner of the earth, every nationality, every race, every language: I love you from the bottom of my heart. I would love your prayers and your goodwill, and please be patient and be with me and believe in me because I am completely, completely innocent. But please know a lot of conspiracy is going on as we speak.
— Michael Jackson

Marlon Brando has been pushing. He's a wonderful man. He's a god. He wants a lot of money. He wants to get things done right now. - On a video about acting which he was planning to make with Brando in 2001
— Michael Jackson

Elizabeth Taylor is a warm cuddly blanket that I love to snuggle up to and cover myself with. I can confide in

her and trust her. She's Mother Teresa, Princess Diana, the Queen of England, and Wendy.
— Michael Jackson

I was coming out of the shower and I fell and all my body weight - I'm pretty fragile - all my body weight fell against my rib cage. And I bruised my lung very badly.
— Michael Jackson

I love my children. I was holding my son tight. Why would I throw a baby off the balcony? That's the dumbest, stupidest story I ever heard.
— Michael Jackson

I think that it's demeaning and disrespectful but I also want to make it clear it's not just about me but a pattern of disrespect that he has shown to our community. He needs to stop it and he needs to stop it now. - On Eminem's video for Just Lose It
— Michael Jackson

I have spent my entire life helping millions of children across the world. I would never harm a child. It is unfortunate that some individuals have seen fit to come forward and make a complaint that is completely false. Years ago, I settled with certain individuals because I was concerned about my family and the media scrutiny that would have ensued if I fought the matter in court. These people wanted to exploit my concern for children by threatening to destroy what I believe in and what I do. I have been a vulnerable target for those who want money.

— Michael Jackson

I am always writing a potpourri of music. I want to give the world escapism through the wonder of great music and to reach the masses.

— Michael Jackson

I'm a visionary and a creative person. God blessed me with certain talents. I hate to use an analogy, but Walt Disney was creative but not good with business. His brother Roy handled the books. He loved creating family-oriented entertainment and so do I. I feel that was a gift and I have that gift also. I'm very honored to have been chosen.

— Michael Jackson

When I saw him move I was mesmerized. I've never seen a performer perform like James Brown and right then and there I knew that that was what I wanted to do for the rest of my life.
— Michael Jackson

Success definitely brings on loneliness. People think you're lucky, that you have everything. They think you can go anywhere and do anything, but that's not the point. One hungers for the basic stuff.
— Michael Jackson

My father was a management genius. But what I really wanted was a dad.
— Michael Jackson

I've been in the entertainment industry since I was six-years-old ... As Charles Dickens says, 'It's been the best of times, the worst of times.' But I would not change my career ... While some have made deliberate attempts to hurt me, I take it in stride because I have a loving family, a strong faith and wonderful friends and fans who have, and continue, to support me.
— Michael Jackson

It all went by so fast, didn't it? I wish I could do it all over again, I really do.
— Michael Jackson

[on refuting persistent rumors of skin surgery or bleaching] If I had a chance to talk to Michelangelo, I would ask him what inspired him to become who he is, the anatomy of his craftsmanship, not about who he dated last night or why he decided to sit out in the sun so long.
— Michael Jackson

When I was 16, we were doing Las Vegas every night, and Elvis Presley and Sammy Davis Jr. would sit me and my brothers in a row and lecture us. 'Don't ever do drugs,' they told us. I never forgot it.
— Michael Jackson

Music has been my outlet, my gift to all of the lovers in this world. Through it, my music, I know I will live forever.
— Michael Jackson

You have to have that tragedy, that pain to pull from. That's what makes a clown great. You can see he's hurting behind the masquerade. He's something else externally. Charles Chaplin did that so beautifully, better than anyone. I can play off those moments, too. I've been through the fire many times.
— Michael Jackson

I never had the chance to do the fun things kids do: sleepovers, parties, trick-or-treat. There was no Christmas, no holiday celebrating. So now you try to compensate for some of that loss.
— Michael Jackson

My father is a much nicer person now. I think he realizes his children are everything. Without your family, you have nothing. He's a nice human being. At one time, we'd be horrified if he just showed up. We were scared to death. He turned out really well. I wish it wasn't so late.
— Michael Jackson

I'm still fascinated by clouds and the sunset. I was making wishes on the rainbow yesterday. I saw the meteor shower. I made a wish every time I saw a shooting star.

— Michael Jackson

I have confidence in my abilities. I have real perseverance. Nothing can stop me when I put my mind to it.

— Michael Jackson

I never think about themes. I let the music create itself. I like it to be a potpourri of all kinds of sounds, all kinds of colors, something for everybody, from the farmer in Ireland to the lady who scrubs toilets in Harlem.

— Michael Jackson

I've had people come to me, and after meeting me, they start crying. I say, Why are you crying? They say, Because I thought you would be stuck up, but you're the nicest person. I say, Who gave you this judgment? They tell me they read it. I tell them, Don't you believe what you read.

— Michael Jackson

When I'm on stage, it's like a two-hour marathon. I weigh myself before and after each show, and I lose a good 10 pounds. Sweat is all over the stage. Then you get to your hotel and your adrenaline is at its zenith and you can't fall asleep. And you've got a show the next day. It's tough.
— Michael Jackson

I never self-proclaimed myself to be anything. If I called up Elizabeth Taylor right now, she would tell you that she coined the phrase. She was introducing me, I think at the American Music Awards, and said in her own words - it wasn't in the script - I'm a personal fan, and in my opinion he is the king of pop, rock and soul. Then the press started saying King of Pop and the fans started. This self-proclaimed garbage, I don't know who said that.
— Michael Jackson

I sit in my room at home and sometimes cry. It's so hard to make friends. Sometimes I walk around the neighbourhood at night, just hoping to find someone to talk to. But I just end up coming home.
— Michael Jackson

[on being asked what he thought his funeral would be like in 2002] It's going to be the greatest show on Earth. That's what I want. Fireworks and everything.
— Michael Jackson

[on recording in Ireland in 2006] I've never given up on making music. Ireland has inspired me to make a great new album.
— Michael Jackson

If you enter this world knowing you are loved and you leave this world knowing the same, then everything that happens in between can be dealt with.
— Michael Jackson

I am the captain of my ship. I take suggestions and listen to what everyone has to say, but the final decision is mine.
— Michael Jackson

[on his father] He is a very jealous father. He isn't gonna show you love, but anybody that gets closer to us than him he would tell them, 'Leave my boys alone!'

To tell you the truth, I never have felt close to him. He has always been like a mystery man.
— Michael Jackson

I would like some way to disappear where people don't see me anymore at some point. I don't want to grow old. I never want to look in the mirror and see that.
— Michael Jackson

The greatest education in the world is watching the masters at work.
— Michael Jackson

In a world filled with hate, we must still dare to hope. In a world filled with anger, we must still dare to comfort. In a world filled with despair, we must still dare to dream. And in a world filled with distrust, we must still dare to believe.
— Michael Jackson

Why can't you share your bed? The most loving thing you can do is share your bed with someone. It's very

charming. It's very sweet. It's what the whole world should do.
— Michael Jackson

A star can never die. It just turns into a smile and melts back into the cosmic music, the dance of life.
— Michael Jackson

You never know how long you have with someone, so don't forget to say I love you while you can.
— Michael Jackson

I say, 'You should blanket me' or 'you should blanket her', meaning like a blanket is a blessing. It's a way of showing love and caring.
— Michael Jackson

Love is the human family's most precious legacy. Its richest bequest. Its golden inheritance.
— Michael Jackson

For me, Love is something very pure.
— Michael Jackson

Of course, I believe in love. Its beautiful when it's right. My love life is like my music.
— Michael Jackson

Its all for Love.. L.O.V.E.
— Michael Jackson

I'm a gentleman, call me old fashioned if you want.
— Michael Jackson

To me, ballads are special, because you can have a pop song that'll be know for three weeks and then you'll hear nothing else about it. Nobody else will record it and it'll just be gone. But if you do a good ballad, it'll be in the world forever.
— Michael Jackson

To live is to be musical, starting with the blood dancing in your veins. Everything living has a rhythm. Do you feel your music?
— Michael Jackson

When you have a special gift you don't realize it because you think everyone else has the same gift.
— Michael Jackson

I can't take credit for it because its Gods work. He's just using me as the messenger.
— Michael Jackson

To live is to be musical, starting with the blood dancing in your veins. Everything living has a rhythm. Do you feel your music?
— Michael Jackson

Music is a very important and powerful substance, and all the planets in the universe make music. It's called music of the spheres. They all make a different note; they make harmony. So there's harmony even in the universe as we speak.
— Michael Jackson

With my music, with what I do, I would like to bring a light into the world.
— Michael Jackson

Each song is like a child that I nourish and give my love to. But even if you have never written a song, your life is a song.
— Michael Jackson

They say parenting is like dancing. You take one step, and your child takes another.
— Michael Jackson

Once I get on stage, something happens. The rhythm starts and the lights hit me and the problems disappear.
— Michael Jackson

I feel like I've done what I'm supposed to do on Earth..
I'm compelled to do these things.
— Michael Jackson

I love to create. I love to make magic. I love to create the unexpected.
— Michael Jackson

I love to dance and sing.
— Michael Jackson

Im putting my heart and soul into it because Im not sure if Im gonna do another one after this.. This will be my last album.. I want it to be something that touches the heart and emotions of the world. I want to reach every demographic I can through love and joy and simplicity of music.

— Michael Jackson

You give of your talent, of your ability.. The talent that was given you by the Heavens. That's why we're here, to bring a sense of escapism in time of need. If you're a painter you paint; if you're a sculptor, you sculpt; if you're a writer, you write; if you're a songwriter, you give songs; if you're a dancer, you give dance. You give people some love and some... some bliss and some escapism, and to show that you truly care from the heart, and be there for them. Not just from a distance, but show you really care. You be there for them. And that's what I did. It's an important thing.

— Michael Jackson

The songwriting process is something very difficult to explain because it's very spiritual.. You really have it in the hands of God, and it's as if it's been written already

– that's the real truth. As if it's been written in its entirety before were born and you're just really the source through which the songs come.. And I feel guilty having to put my name, sometimes, on the songs that.. I do write them. I compose them, I write them, I do the scoring, I do the lyrics, I do the melodies but still.. It's a work of God.
— Michael Jackson

Music has been my outlet, my gift to all of the lovers in this world. Through it, I know I will live forever.
— Michael Jackson

Forever, continue to love, heal and educate the children, the future shines on them.
— Michael Jackson

Nothing is more important than our children. They are the future. They can heal the world. It is our obligation to be there for them.
— Michael Jackson

I think its important to help out as much as you can.
Just to help one person means a lot. Its a big step
forward.
— Michael Jackson

Start with the man in the mirror. Start with yourself.
Dont be looking at all the other things. Start with you
— Michael Jackson

We listen, we watch, we learn. We open our hearts, and
we open our minds.
— Michael Jackson

Be humble, believe in yourself, and have the love of the
world in your heart.
— Michael Jackson

The only reason I'm going on tour is to raise for the
newly formed, 'Heal The World', an international
children's charity, that I'm spearheading to assist
children and the ecology. My goal is to gross $100
million by Christmas, 1993. I urge every corporation
and individual who cares about this planet and the
future of the children, to help raise money for the HTW

charity. The Heal The World Foundation will contribute funds to pediatric aids in honor of my friend, Ryan White. I'm looking forward to this tour, because it will allow me to devote time to visiting children all around the world, as well as to spread the message of the global love, in the hopes that others too will be moved to do their share to heal the world. Thank you for coming. I love you very much.

— Michael Jackson

I'm saying heal the planet, heal the world, save our children, save the forest. There is nothing wrong with that, right?

— Michael Jackson

I have spent my entire life helping millions of children across the world.

— Michael Jackson

Just let me share and give, put a smile on people's faces and make their hearts feel happy.

— Michael Jackson

God gave me a gift & I have to use it responsibly by giving back. I'll do it until I have pennies left or God calls me home.
— Michael Jackson

For me the sweetest contact with God has no form. I close my eyes, look within.. The infinity of God's creation embraces me
— Michael Jackson

There have been times in my life when I wonder[ed] about God's existence. When Prince smiles, when Paris giggles, I have no doubts.
— Michael Jackson

I try to be kind and generous, and to give to people, and to do what I think God wants me to do.
— Michael Jackson

I see God through my children. I speak to God through my children. I am humbled for the blessings He has given me.
— Michael Jackson

I truly love my fans. Truly, truly from the heart. That's the real truth. I love them.
— Michael Jackson

I promise To love and cherish each of my sweet-faced fans forever..
— Michael Jackson

I just do what I do & I love doing it. I pray that Im doing my job, what I'm here to do on Earth.. Because I love the fans.
— Michael Jackson

Over the years we became a family. You are all my family. My children are your children.
— Michael Jackson

I love my fans to pieces. They're with me. They get it, you know? They get what I'm saying.
— Michael Jackson

I have the greatest fans in the world. I love them.. All of them, I really do.
— Michael Jackson

My fans.. They cry in all the same places. Become hysterical, faint in the same places. There is a commonality. We are all the same.
— Michael Jackson

I don't believe in the justice system. I have seen things go on in the world & how people get away with them
— Michael Jackson

God and the truth are on our side. We will be victorious.
— Michael Jackson

My level of trust will change. There's a lot of conspiracy going on, I'll say that much. A lot of it.
— Michael Jackson

I have suffered through many hurtful lies and references to me as 'Wacko Jacko'... This is intolerable and must stop.
— Michael Jackson

You have to deal with their jealousy. They're all talking about you. When they stop talking, you have to worry.
— Michael Jackson

Sometimes I think leave me alone. What have I done to you for you to attack me in such away. It really hurts my heart
— Michael Jackson

In my business you cant trust anyone because you don't know who's your friend. Becoming successful means you become a prisoner
— Michael Jackson

I have been a vulnerable target for those who want money.
— Michael Jackson

I missed out on Halloween for years and now I do it. It's sweet to go door-to-door & people give you candy.
— Michael Jackson

I love to trick or treat... I love dressing up like some kind of monster... and knocking on doors. Nobody knows it's me and I get candy.
— Michael Jackson

I always thought Halloween and 'Thriller' fit each other like a glove.
— Michael Jackson

The essence of Halloween is for children to witness the kindness of strangers.. It brings the world together.
— Michael Jackson

I cry behind my mask.I really do when I go w/ them&ppl say,Open ur bag, & I think,look what I hv been missing.I didn't know that this.
— Michael Jackson

I love trick or treat. It's one of my favorite ones.
— Michael Jackson

I love dressing up like some kind of monster or

something and knocking on the doors. Nobody knows it's me, and I get candy.

— Michael Jackson

It's sweet to go door-to-door and people give you candy. We need more of that in the world. It brings the world together.

— Michael Jackson

www.ingramcontent.com/pod-product-compliance
Lightning Source LLC
Chambersburg PA
CBHW071243280526
45788CB00004B/1562